Think & Live Like A Bride

Your Guide to Planning & Living Your Life with Joy!

Copyright © 2022

Praisem Worldwide Publishing

Published in the United States.

ISBN – 979-8-218-09883-4

Author: Cherisse Stephens

Think & Live Like A Bride

Your Guide to Planning & Living Your Life with Joy!

Welcome to Think & Live Like A Bride, the ultimate guide to planning and living your life with Joy! Let me first start out by saying that this guide is for ANYONE who wants to live their lives in JOY. There is no criteria required to get the full benefits from this life planner other than commitment. You must be committed to the process to get the best results for your life.

Think of this guide as a road trip. For the next 12 months, you will go on an excursion to discover how to live your BEST LIFE! I chose this title, **"Think & Live Like A Bride,"** because of the work that most BRIDES do to plan their special day. They have a vision of what that day will look and feel like, and nothing will get in their way to stop it from happening. So whether you are married, divorced, single, young, or old, this planner will help you rediscover your passion for life. Get ready for the journey, your destination is JOY. BUT… make sure you enjoy each moment and each day. Why? It is all a part of the Big Picture.

WELCOME TO YOUR BRIDAL SUITE

NAME OF BRIDE-TO-BE: _____

Let's Get Started

The first thing you need to do on this journey is to focus on the Big Picture. What do you want your life to look like a year from now? Let me say, that this planner is not to say that you are not living a life of peace and joy already. I do want you to be grateful for the space and place that you are in. But, just like the Bride who is planning their special day, there is so much more joy awaiting you.

Let's start by celebrating where you are right now! You've worked hard to get to this point. Stop and take time to reflect on the wonderful things happening in your life. I encourage you to have a party all by yourself. Of course there will be other parties with your family, and friends, but today, it's all about YOU! There is nobody to impress, you do not have to plan food, venue, guest list or any of the other details needed for this special event. This party is you, looking in the mirror of your life and celebrating where you are. Go ahead and write down your accomplishments here:

_____

_____

_____

_____

_____

_____

_____

_____

_____

_____

_____

_____

_____

_____

_____

_____

_____

_____

_____

_____

_____

_____

_____

_____

_____

_____

_____

Don't you feel better? It is important that you Love yourself and the life you've been given. It says that you are ready to discover all the other blessings that are coming your way. All right let's get the LIFE Party Started.

When the BRIDE-TO-BE is planning her BIG DAY, at first, they are excited, overwhelmed, and scared. However, this planner is going to alleviate all of that as you take your time to discover new ways to get to the JOY you so deserve. Your checklist will be a little different from the traditional bride. How so you ask? Well, for one, there are no rules as to how you achieve this goal. Your journey is different from others. So, you don't have to frustrate yourself comparing your path to anyone else. Isn't that awesome? You will discover that your path is designed for you only. This planner is just a guide to help lead you along the way. You can start at Month 12 and work your way to the BIG DAY, or you may opt to start at Month 10 or 6! It's up to you.

The goal is to get to a place where you notice transformation. You'll get there, one day, one hour, one minute, and one second at a time. Enjoy your journey. Be intentional every day about implementing the necessary steps to get to your destination – JOY!

MONTH 12 – LET'S GET THIS LIFE PARTY STARTED!

Now that you understand what this planner is all about, it's time to let others know that you're thinking differently about yourself. For example, remember how excited you were when you started a new exercise routine, or took up a new hobby? You told your family and close friends, so that they could either hold you accountable, or encourage you along the way. Well, this journey is no different. Share with someone about the NEW path you're taking. Let them in on your transformation journey or even better, encourage them to do it with you. Like a Bride, having close family and friends around to celebrate your accomplishments is vital. You're not alone!

Name Your Celebrators i.e. Bride Tribe below. These are the people you trust to celebrate your milestones and encourage you when things get a little rocky. They understand that you deserve all the Goodness that's coming your way. Be careful who you select. If you have reservations about them and what they will contribute to your journey, then perhaps they are not the ones to have on your roster. Let them look from afar and witness the transformation. It's Okay, you still have relationship with them, but this journey is too important to take extra baggage with you! It may cost you too much.

Celebrators (BRIDE TRIBE)

_____

_____

_____

_____

_____

_____

_____

Once you have selected your Celebrators, you are now ready to continue your journey. Most BRIDES will start envisioning what they want their BIG Day to look like. What type of dress, shoes, hair style, etc.... So much goes into planning the BIG DAY. Well, it's the same for your BIG Day as well. You have to Vision what 12 months or 6 months from now will look like for you. How are you going to do that? A Vision Board! That's right, you're going to create a vision board that speaks to your future. Remember to think Like A Bride so you can Live like a Bride. Simply meaning that your well-planned life will yield results that will bring you Joy on the BIG DAY and beyond. Are you ready?

BRIDE-TO-BE TO DO LIST: (Check Off When Completed)

1.

2.

3.

4.

5.

THINK AND LIVE LIKE A BRIDE NOTES

_____
_____
_____
_____
_____
_____
_____
_____
_____
_____
_____
_____
_____
_____

BRIDE-TO-BE TO DO LIST: (Check Off When Completed)

1.

2.

3.

4.

5.

THINK AND LIVE LIKE A BRIDE NOTES

_____
_____
_____
_____
_____
_____
_____
_____
_____
_____
_____
_____
_____
_____

BRIDE-TO-BE TO DO LIST: (Check Off When Completed)

1.

2.

3.

4.

5.

THINK AND LIVE LIKE A BRIDE NOTES

_____

_____

_____

_____

_____

_____

_____

_____

_____

_____

_____

_____

_____

_____

BRIDE-TO-BE TO DO LIST: (Check Off When Completed)

1.

2.

3.

4.

5.

THINK AND LIVE LIKE A BRIDE NOTES

_____
_____
_____
_____
_____
_____
_____
_____
_____
_____
_____
_____
_____

BRIDE-TO-BE TO DO LIST: (Check Off When Completed)

1.

2.

3.

4.

5.

THINK AND LIVE LIKE A BRIDE NOTES

_____

_____

_____

_____

_____

_____

_____

_____

_____

_____

_____

_____

_____

BRIDE-TO-BE TO DO LIST: (Check Off When Completed)

1.

2.

3.

4.

5.

THINK AND LIVE LIKE A BRIDE NOTES

_____

_____

_____

_____

_____

_____

_____

_____

_____

_____

_____

_____

BRIDE-TO-BE TO DO LIST: (Check Off When Completed)

1.

2.

3.

4.

5.

THINK AND LIVE LIKE A BRIDE NOTES

_____
_____
_____
_____
_____
_____
_____
_____
_____
_____
_____
_____
_____
_____

BRIDE-TO-BE TO DO LIST: (Check Off When Completed)

1.

2.

3.

4.

5.

THINK AND LIVE LIKE A BRIDE NOTES

_____

_____

_____

_____

_____

_____

_____

_____

_____

_____

_____

_____

_____

BRIDE-TO-BE TO DO LIST: (Check Off When Completed)

1.

2.

3.

4.

5.

THINK AND LIVE LIKE A BRIDE NOTES

_____
_____
_____
_____
_____
_____
_____
_____
_____
_____
_____
_____
_____

BRIDE-TO-BE TO DO LIST: (Check Off When Completed)

1.

2.

3.

4.

5.

_____
_____
_____
_____
_____
_____
_____
_____
_____
_____
_____
_____
_____
_____

MONTH 11 – STRENGTHS

Let's start this Vision Board off with your Strengths. What are some of the strengths you possess today? Write about them below.

_____
_____
_____
_____
_____
_____

Why did I have you write about your Strengths First? Well think about it, most Brides think about how great they will look on their big day. They think about their beautiful skin tone, or figure. They pick a dress that will compliment them, etc. I want you to think about what an awesome person you already are. Think about all the great qualities you possess. I see you smiling! You should, you deserve to be celebrated. Now let's add to your list. What other qualities would you love to have? Write them below.

_____

_____

_____

_____

_____

_____

_____

I see you BRIDE! (Figuratively speaking of course or maybe not) At any rate, you will become stronger on this journey! You've already started working out. Yes, you're working the biggest muscle you have, your BRAIN! You've already started thinking differently about you and it Shows.

BRIDE-TO-BE TO DO LIST: (Check Off When Completed)

1.

2.

3.

4.

5.

THINK AND LIVE LIKE A BRIDE NOTES

_____
_____
_____
_____
_____
_____
_____
_____
_____
_____
_____
_____
_____

BRIDE-TO-BE TO DO LIST: (Check Off When Completed)

1.

2.

3.

4.

5.

THINK AND LIVE LIKE A BRIDE NOTES

_____

_____

_____

_____

_____

_____

_____

_____

_____

_____

_____

_____

_____

BRIDE-TO-BE TO DO LIST: (Check Off When Completed)

1.

2.

3.

4.

5.

THINK AND LIVE LIKE A BRIDE NOTES

_____
_____
_____
_____
_____
_____
_____
_____
_____
_____
_____
_____
_____
_____

BRIDE-TO-BE TO DO LIST: (Check Off When Completed)

1.

2.

3.

4.

5.

THINK AND LIVE LIKE A BRIDE NOTES

_____

_____

_____

_____

_____

_____

_____

_____

_____

_____

_____

_____

_____

_____

BRIDE-TO-BE TO DO LIST: (Check Off When Completed)

1.

2.

3.

4.

5.

THINK AND LIVE LIKE A BRIDE NOTES

_____
_____
_____
_____
_____
_____
_____
_____
_____
_____
_____
_____
_____
_____

BRIDE-TO-BE TO DO LIST: (Check Off When Completed)

1.

2.

3.

4.

5.

THINK AND LIVE LIKE A BRIDE NOTES

_____

_____

_____

_____

_____

_____

_____

_____

_____

_____

_____

_____

_____

BRIDE-TO-BE TO DO LIST: (Check Off When Completed)

1.

2.

3.

4.

5.

THINK AND LIVE LIKE A BRIDE NOTES

_____
_____
_____
_____
_____
_____
_____
_____
_____
_____
_____
_____
_____

BRIDE-TO-BE TO DO LIST: (Check Off When Completed)

1.

2.

3.

4.

5.

THINK AND LIVE LIKE A BRIDE NOTES

_____

_____

_____

_____

_____

_____

_____

_____

_____

_____

_____

_____

_____

_____

BRIDE-TO-BE TO DO LIST: (Check Off When Completed)

1.

2.

3.

4.

5.

THINK AND LIVE LIKE A BRIDE NOTES

_____

_____

_____

_____

_____

_____

_____

_____

_____

_____

_____

_____

BRIDE-TO-BE TO DO LIST: (Check Off When Completed)

1.

2.

3.

4.

5.

THINK AND LIVE LIKE A BRIDE NOTES

_____

_____

_____

_____

_____

_____

_____

_____

_____

_____

_____

_____

MONTH 10 – WEAKNESSES

I hate to disappoint you, but everyone has a weakness. Even the BRIDE, you see you in your favorite magazine, has some type of battle she must face. You know the person you look up to who has it all together? They too have some weaknesses that they must work on as well. But don't beat yourself up about this area. Remember, this is your VISION Board. Nobody sees you more than you do. You are the only one reflecting back from the mirror you're looking in. You must be truthful about you to get the results you desire. Have you ever gone to try on a dress and selected the dress that was a little too snug hoping you'll be able to fit it on a future date? Well, you also know if you didn't do the work to fit into that dress, your weakness for the ice cream cone or macaroni and cheese would show up! Share your weaknesses below.

_____
_____
_____
_____
_____
_____
_____

What will you do to help overcome your weaknesses?

_____
_____
_____
_____
_____
_____
_____
_____
_____

CONGRATS! You're thinking more Like A Bride! Celebrate the fact that you're NOT perfect, but that you're committed to living and being the BEST version of yourself.

BRIDE-TO-BE TO DO LIST: (Check Off When Completed)

1.

2.

3.

4.

5.

THINK AND LIVE LIKE A BRIDE NOTES

_____

_____

_____

_____

_____

_____

_____

_____

_____

_____

_____

_____

_____

_____

BRIDE-TO-BE TO DO LIST: (Check Off When Completed)

1.

2.

3.

4.

5.

THINK AND LIVE LIKE A BRIDE NOTES

_____
_____
_____
_____
_____
_____
_____
_____
_____
_____
_____
_____
_____

BRIDE-TO-BE TO DO LIST: (Check Off When Completed)

1.

2.

3.

4.

5.

THINK AND LIVE LIKE A BRIDE NOTES

_____

_____

_____

_____

_____

_____

_____

_____

_____

_____

_____

_____

_____

BRIDE-TO-BE TO DO LIST: (Check Off When Completed)

1.

2.

3.

4.

5.

THINK AND LIVE LIKE A BRIDE NOTES

_____
_____
_____
_____
_____
_____
_____
_____
_____
_____
_____
_____
_____

BRIDE-TO-BE TO DO LIST: (Check Off When Completed)

1.

2.

3.

4.

5.

THINK AND LIVE LIKE A BRIDE NOTES

_____
_____
_____
_____
_____
_____
_____
_____
_____
_____
_____
_____
_____
_____
_____

BRIDE-TO-BE TO DO LIST: (Check Off When Completed)

1.

2.

3.

4.

5.

THINK AND LIVE LIKE A BRIDE NOTES

_____

_____

_____

_____

_____

_____

_____

_____

_____

_____

_____

_____

_____

BRIDE-TO-BE TO DO LIST: (Check Off When Completed)

1.

2.

3.

4.

5.

THINK AND LIVE LIKE A BRIDE NOTES

_____
_____
_____
_____
_____
_____
_____
_____
_____
_____
_____
_____
_____
_____

BRIDE-TO-BE TO DO LIST: (Check Off When Completed)

1.

2.

3.

4.

5.

THINK AND LIVE LIKE A BRIDE NOTES

_____
_____
_____
_____
_____
_____
_____
_____
_____
_____
_____
_____

BRIDE-TO-BE TO DO LIST: (Check Off When Completed)

1.

2.

3.

4.

5.

THINK AND LIVE LIKE A BRIDE NOTES

_____

_____

_____

_____

_____

_____

_____

_____

_____

_____

_____

_____

_____

BRIDE-TO-BE TO DO LIST: (Check Off When Completed)

1.

2.

3.

4.

5.

THINK AND LIVE LIKE A BRIDE NOTES

_____

_____

_____

_____

_____

_____

_____

_____

_____

_____

_____

_____

MONTH 9 – OPPORTUNITIES

Just like the happy bride, you get the OPPORTUNITY to plan your life with JOY. In doing so, you will get to encounter what I call "Divine Connections." Your path will allow you to connect to people who can assist you on your journey to wholeness. Let's consider the BRIDE'S journey to the Big Day, she realizes that she can't do it alone. She will need a photographer, videographer, wedding planner, florist, musicians, singers, officiant, GROOM and so much more. Each person has a specific role that will enhance the BRIDE'S Big Day! Well, you no longer have to wish it were you walking down the aisle. You're going to take this walk every day. How amazing is that? You get the opportunity to "choose" those who will play significant roles in your life. There will also be those who are referred to you or sent into your life to enhance it. Your steps are divinely ordered, and your life will come into divine alignment when you focus on the path that is set before you.

What opportunities do you want to encounter on your Journey to Joy?

_____

_____

_____

_____

_____

_____

_____

_____

_____

_____

You should be proud of the work you're doing to get to the life you want to live. Take every opportunity and use it to your advantage. These opportunities are designed to benefit you and those who are connected to you.

BRIDE-TO-BE TO DO LIST: (Check Off When Completed)

1.

2.

3.

4.

5.

THINK AND LIVE LIKE A BRIDE NOTES

_____

_____

_____

_____

_____

_____

_____

_____

_____

_____

_____

_____

BRIDE-TO-BE TO DO LIST: (Check Off When Completed)

1.

2.

3.

4.

5.

THINK AND LIVE LIKE A BRIDE NOTES

_____
_____
_____
_____
_____
_____
_____
_____
_____
_____
_____
_____
_____
_____

BRIDE-TO-BE TO DO LIST: (Check Off When Completed)

1.

2.

3.

4.

5.

THINK AND LIVE LIKE A BRIDE NOTES

_____
_____
_____
_____
_____
_____
_____
_____
_____
_____
_____
_____
_____

BRIDE-TO-BE TO DO LIST: (Check Off When Completed)

1.

2.

3.

4.

5.

THINK AND LIVE LIKE A BRIDE NOTES

_____
_____
_____
_____
_____
_____
_____
_____
_____
_____
_____
_____
_____
_____

BRIDE-TO-BE TO DO LIST: (Check Off When Completed)

1.

2.

3.

4.

5.

THINK AND LIVE LIKE A BRIDE NOTES

_____

_____

_____

_____

_____

_____

_____

_____

_____

_____

_____

_____

BRIDE-TO-BE TO DO LIST: (Check Off When Completed)

1.

2.

3.

4.

5.

THINK AND LIVE LIKE A BRIDE NOTES

_____

_____

_____

_____

_____

_____

_____

_____

_____

_____

_____

_____

_____

BRIDE-TO-BE TO DO LIST: (Check Off When Completed)

1.

2.

3.

4.

5.

THINK AND LIVE LIKE A BRIDE NOTES

_____
_____
_____
_____
_____
_____
_____
_____
_____
_____
_____
_____

BRIDE-TO-BE TO DO LIST: (Check Off When Completed)

1.

2.

3.

4.

5.

THINK AND LIVE LIKE A BRIDE NOTES

_____
_____
_____
_____
_____
_____
_____
_____
_____
_____
_____
_____
_____
_____

BRIDE-TO-BE TO DO LIST: (Check Off When Completed)

1.

2.

3.

4.

5.

THINK AND LIVE LIKE A BRIDE NOTES

_____

_____

_____

_____

_____

_____

_____

_____

_____

_____

_____

_____

BRIDE-TO-BE TO DO LIST: (Check Off When Completed)

1.

2.

3.

4.

5.

_____

_____

_____

_____

_____

_____

_____

_____

_____

_____

_____

_____

MONTH 8 – THREATS

BRIDE-TO-BE – I do have an announcement. There will be some things to come your way to threaten your life of JOY! Unfortunately, there will be people who envy this path that you are on. YOU must remain focused as you plan and implement what is in your heart concerning your life. When I think of a Bride-To-Be, one of their biggest threats is "gaining weight." They have a fear of not being able to fit into the beautiful dress that they have selected for their Big Day! So they are intentional about what and when they eat. You must also take this approach when you are planning your life. Be careful not to eat things like negativity, jealousy, competition, disappointment, and other things to distract you. Too many of these attributes will most likely cause you to gain weight. You'll be carrying baggage that's too heavy for where you're going. Eat things that bring you peace and joy.

Name some things that you will digest on your journey to enhance you!

_____

_____

_____

_____

_____

_____

_____

_____

_____

_____

YOUR LIFE IS SHAPING UP NICELY...KEEP GOING!

BRIDE-TO-BE TO DO LIST: (Check Off When Completed)

1.

2.

3.

4.

5.

THINK AND LIVE LIKE A BRIDE NOTES

_____

_____

_____

_____

_____

_____

_____

_____

_____

_____

_____

_____

_____

BRIDE-TO-BE TO DO LIST: (Check Off When Completed)

1.

2.

3.

4.

5.

THINK AND LIVE LIKE A BRIDE NOTES

_____
_____
_____
_____
_____
_____
_____
_____
_____
_____
_____
_____
_____

BRIDE-TO-BE TO DO LIST: (Check Off When Completed)

1.

2.

3.

4.

5.

THINK AND LIVE LIKE A BRIDE NOTES

_____
_____
_____
_____
_____
_____
_____
_____
_____
_____
_____
_____
_____
_____

BRIDE-TO-BE TO DO LIST: (Check Off When Completed)

1.

2.

3.

4.

5.

THINK AND LIVE LIKE A BRIDE NOTES

_____

_____

_____

_____

_____

_____

_____

_____

_____

_____

_____

_____

_____

BRIDE-TO-BE TO DO LIST: (Check Off When Completed)

1.

2.

3.

4.

5.

THINK AND LIVE LIKE A BRIDE NOTES

_____

_____

_____

_____

_____

_____

_____

_____

_____

_____

_____

_____

_____

_____

BRIDE-TO-BE TO DO LIST: (Check Off When Completed)

1.

2.

3.

4.

5.

THINK AND LIVE LIKE A BRIDE NOTES

_____
_____
_____
_____
_____
_____
_____
_____
_____
_____
_____
_____
_____

BRIDE-TO-BE TO DO LIST: (Check Off When Completed)

1.

2.

3.

4.

5.

THINK AND LIVE LIKE A BRIDE NOTES

_____
_____
_____
_____
_____
_____
_____
_____
_____
_____
_____
_____
_____

BRIDE-TO-BE TO DO LIST: (Check Off When Completed)

1.

2.

3.

4.

5.

THINK AND LIVE LIKE A BRIDE NOTES

_____

_____

_____

_____

_____

_____

_____

_____

_____

_____

_____

_____

BRIDE-TO-BE TO DO LIST: (Check Off When Completed)

1.

2.

3.

4.

5.

THINK AND LIVE LIKE A BRIDE NOTES

_____
_____
_____
_____
_____
_____
_____
_____
_____
_____
_____
_____
_____

BRIDE-TO-BE TO DO LIST: (Check Off When Completed)

1.

2.

3.

4.

5.

_____

_____

_____

_____

_____

_____

_____

_____

_____

_____

_____

_____

MONTH 7 - JOY FOR THE JOURNEY!

I had to ask this question, because like so many Brides-To-Be, on their journey to the BIG DAY, they forget to have FUN! They get so boggled down with the details, that they forget that this path is supposed to bring joy throughout the process. There was a story of a man who planned a trip to go on a cruise to a certain country. He was extremely excited about the trip; however, he didn't have much money after paying for the trip. So every day, he would eat from a packed lunch that he brought with him. He would look at the other passengers and WISH he could eat with them. One day, one of his fellow passengers saw him eating from his brown paper bag. They asked him why he wasn't enjoying the limitless buffet of exquisite foods and drink. He replied by saying, "I thought I had to pay EXTRA for that." He didn't realize that the buffet was inclusive of the price he had already paid! Can you imagine the JOY he had when he found out that he too could eat and enjoy all that was surrounding him? He decided from that point on to enjoy the Journey, not just the destination.

What are you doing to enjoy the journey?

_____
_____
_____
_____
_____
_____
_____
_____
_____
_____

ENJOY THE JOURNEY, NOT JUST THE DESTINATION.

BRIDE-TO-BE TO DO LIST: (Check Off When Completed)

1.

2.

3.

4.

5.

THINK AND LIVE LIKE A BRIDE NOTES

_____

_____

_____

_____

_____

_____

_____

_____

_____

_____

_____

_____

BRIDE-TO-BE TO DO LIST: (Check Off When Completed)

1.

2.

3.

4.

5.

THINK AND LIVE LIKE A BRIDE NOTES

_____
_____
_____
_____
_____
_____
_____
_____
_____
_____
_____
_____
_____
_____

BRIDE-TO-BE TO DO LIST: (Check Off When Completed)

1.

2.

3.

4.

5.

THINK AND LIVE LIKE A BRIDE NOTES

_____
_____
_____
_____
_____
_____
_____
_____
_____
_____
_____
_____

BRIDE-TO-BE TO DO LIST: (Check Off When Completed)

1.

2.

3.

4.

5.

THINK AND LIVE LIKE A BRIDE NOTES

_____
_____
_____
_____
_____
_____
_____
_____
_____
_____
_____
_____
_____

BRIDE-TO-BE TO DO LIST: (Check Off When Completed)

1.

2.

3.

4.

5.

THINK AND LIVE LIKE A BRIDE NOTES

_____

_____

_____

_____

_____

_____

_____

_____

_____

_____

_____

_____

BRIDE-TO-BE TO DO LIST: (Check Off When Completed)

1.

2.

3.

4.

5.

THINK AND LIVE LIKE A BRIDE NOTES

_____

_____

_____

_____

_____

_____

_____

_____

_____

_____

_____

_____

_____

BRIDE-TO-BE TO DO LIST: (Check Off When Completed)

1.

2.

3.

4.

5.

THINK AND LIVE LIKE A BRIDE NOTES

_____

_____

_____

_____

_____

_____

_____

_____

_____

_____

_____

_____

BRIDE-TO-BE TO DO LIST: (Check Off When Completed)

1.

2.

3.

4.

5.

THINK AND LIVE LIKE A BRIDE NOTES

_____
_____
_____
_____
_____
_____
_____
_____
_____
_____
_____
_____
_____
_____

BRIDE-TO-BE TO DO LIST: (Check Off When Completed)

1.

2.

3.

4.

5.

THINK AND LIVE LIKE A BRIDE NOTES

_____

_____

_____

_____

_____

_____

_____

_____

_____

_____

_____

_____

BRIDE-TO-BE TO DO LIST: (Check Off When Completed)

1.

2.

3.

4.

5.

THINK AND LIVE LIKE A BRIDE NOTES

MONTH 6 – SAVE THE DATE

You should be super proud of all the accomplishments you have achieved in the past 6 months of your life. You've been intentional about changing things and bringing JOY to your Journey. When a Bride-To-Be is planning her Big Day, she wants everyone to know that her life is changing, and you should too. She will send out the Save The Date cards to people who are important to her and the groom. The Save The Date announcement is to let others in on their JOY. Remember, we are "thinking like a bride," so you should do the same in your own life starting today. For example, have you ever gone on a diet, and people who haven't seen you in a long time respond to you in such a way that is shocking to them and you? They ask you all kinds of questions, like how did you do it, how long did it take, what did you eat? The questions are endless and the stares you receive are quite entertaining. Go ahead and let others in on your Joy Journey. They already see that your life has shifted into something greater. They are trying to figure it out! It's time to let them in on your JOY secrets. Most times when this happens, others will hop on the JOY wagon. They'll want to experience it for themselves. In fact, that's what this is all about. You get the opportunity to bring others along for the ride. **How will you Announce Your Transformation?**

What will your SAVE The DATE Say?

WHO: _____

WHAT:

_____

_____

WHEN:

_____

WHERE:

_____

BRIDE-TO-BE TO DO LIST: (Check Off When Completed)

1.

2.

3.

4.

5.

THINK AND LIVE LIKE A BRIDE NOTES

_____
_____
_____
_____
_____
_____
_____
_____
_____
_____
_____
_____
_____

BRIDE-TO-BE TO DO LIST: (Check Off When Completed)

1.

2.

3.

4.

5.

THINK AND LIVE LIKE A BRIDE NOTES

_____

_____

_____

_____

_____

_____

_____

_____

_____

_____

_____

_____

BRIDE-TO-BE TO DO LIST: (Check Off When Completed)

1.

2.

3.

4.

5.

THINK AND LIVE LIKE A BRIDE NOTES

_____
_____
_____
_____
_____
_____
_____
_____
_____
_____
_____
_____
_____

BRIDE-TO-BE TO DO LIST: (Check Off When Completed)

1.

2.

3.

4.

5.

THINK AND LIVE LIKE A BRIDE NOTES

_____
_____
_____
_____
_____
_____
_____
_____
_____
_____
_____
_____
_____

BRIDE-TO-BE TO DO LIST: (Check Off When Completed)

1.

2.

3.

4.

5.

THINK AND LIVE LIKE A BRIDE NOTES

_____

_____

_____

_____

_____

_____

_____

_____

_____

_____

_____

_____

_____

BRIDE-TO-BE TO DO LIST: (Check Off When Completed)

1.

2.

3.

4.

5.

THINK AND LIVE LIKE A BRIDE NOTES

_____

_____

_____

_____

_____

_____

_____

_____

_____

_____

_____

_____

BRIDE-TO-BE TO DO LIST: (Check Off When Completed)

1.

2.

3.

4.

5.

THINK AND LIVE LIKE A BRIDE NOTES

_____

_____

_____

_____

_____

_____

_____

_____

_____

_____

_____

_____

_____

_____

BRIDE-TO-BE TO DO LIST: (Check Off When Completed)

1.

2.

3.

4.

5.

THINK AND LIVE LIKE A BRIDE NOTES

_____
_____
_____
_____
_____
_____
_____
_____
_____
_____
_____
_____
_____

BRIDE-TO-BE TO DO LIST: (Check Off When Completed)

1.

2.

3.

4.

5.

THINK AND LIVE LIKE A BRIDE NOTES

_____

_____

_____

_____

_____

_____

_____

_____

_____

_____

_____

_____

BRIDE-TO-BE TO DO LIST: (Check Off When Completed)

1.

2.

3.

4.

5.

_____

_____

_____

_____

_____

_____

_____

_____

_____

_____

_____

MONTH 5 – GIVE YOURSELF SOME GRACE

Go back and re-visit your vision board. Remember all the awesome goals you set for yourself? While you have accomplished much, don't be too hard on yourself if you still have lots of things to accomplish. Just like the BRIDE who plans her Big DAY, there will be some things that just don't get done in the timeframe you wished for. It's okay to extend GRACE to yourself. Look in that same mirror that you made all the positive affirmations about your life and tell yourself, it's OKAY! Remember, it takes a village to help you on this JOY Journey. You don't have to do this by yourself; you are not alone. Pull on your Bride Tribe to help you. For example, the photographer and videographer are there to capture all the special moments, the officiant will be there to help you with the ceremony, the caterer is there to provide the food and drinks. Everyone in your life plays a vital role. Use them to your advantage. You'll find that when you do, life can get a little easier. You have been equipped with all the necessary tools to live life with gratitude and grace.

How will you be intentional about showing yourself GRACE?

_____
_____
_____
_____
_____
_____
_____
_____
_____
_____
_____
_____

I'm GRACED for the Journey!

BRIDE-TO-BE TO DO LIST: (Check Off When Completed)

1.

2.

3.

4.

5.

THINK AND LIVE LIKE A BRIDE NOTES

_____

_____

_____

_____

_____

_____

_____

_____

_____

_____

_____

_____

BRIDE-TO-BE TO DO LIST: (Check Off When Completed)

1.

2.

3.

4.

5.

THINK AND LIVE LIKE A BRIDE NOTES

_____
_____
_____
_____
_____
_____
_____
_____
_____
_____
_____
_____
_____

BRIDE-TO-BE TO DO LIST: (Check Off When Completed)

1.

2.

3.

4.

5.

THINK AND LIVE LIKE A BRIDE NOTES

_____

_____

_____

_____

_____

_____

_____

_____

_____

_____

_____

_____

BRIDE-TO-BE TO DO LIST: (Check Off When Completed)

1.

2.

3.

4.

5.

THINK AND LIVE LIKE A BRIDE NOTES

_____
_____
_____
_____
_____
_____
_____
_____
_____
_____
_____
_____

BRIDE-TO-BE TO DO LIST: (Check Off When Completed)

1.

2.

3.

4.

5.

THINK AND LIVE LIKE A BRIDE NOTES

_____

_____

_____

_____

_____

_____

_____

_____

_____

_____

_____

_____

_____

BRIDE-TO-BE TO DO LIST: (Check Off When Completed)

1.

2.

3.

4.

5.

THINK AND LIVE LIKE A BRIDE NOTES

_____
_____
_____
_____
_____
_____
_____
_____
_____
_____
_____
_____
_____

BRIDE-TO-BE TO DO LIST: (Check Off When Completed)

1.

2.

3.

4.

5.

THINK AND LIVE LIKE A BRIDE NOTES

_____
_____
_____
_____
_____
_____
_____
_____
_____
_____
_____
_____
_____

BRIDE-TO-BE TO DO LIST: (Check Off When Completed)

1.

2.

3.

4.

5.

THINK AND LIVE LIKE A BRIDE NOTES

_____
_____
_____
_____
_____
_____
_____
_____
_____
_____
_____
_____
_____

BRIDE-TO-BE TO DO LIST: (Check Off When Completed)

1.

2.

3.

4.

5.

THINK AND LIVE LIKE A BRIDE NOTES

_____
_____
_____
_____
_____
_____
_____
_____
_____
_____
_____
_____
_____

BRIDE-TO-BE TO DO LIST: (Check Off When Completed)

1.

2.

3.

4.

5.

THINK AND LIVE LIKE A BRIDE NOTES

_____
_____
_____
_____
_____
_____
_____
_____
_____
_____
_____
_____

MONTH 4 – WHAT'S YOUR VIBE?

Wonderful things are happening in your life. I see the smile on your face and so does everyone else. I found out that JOY is contagious! When you are intentional about your life, it will spill over to those who are connected to you. Nobody wants to be around the Bridezilla! LOL. The Bridezilla is only concerned about herself. She wants what she wants when she wants it! Your Bride Tribe should enjoy being around you, even though you may be detoxing negativity and so much more. Your journey should bring inspiration and motivation for those who know you or even the person who is watching you from afar.

What is your **BRIDE VIBE?** I love that question! Do a self-check-in to make sure your vibe is positive. Why not take today and do something special for someone else! Gather your "Celebrators" and take them to lunch or dinner. Don't talk to them about your special day. In fact, tell them that talking about your life is off limits today. Find out what they have going on in their lives. Spend quality time listening and being supportive of them. You're going to feel so much better when you do this. Spreading

JOY to others is another crucial step on your journey to JOY. This is the time when the Bride-To-Be is picking dresses, jewelry, shoes, hairstyles for their Bride Tribe. The Bride-To-Be wants to ensure that the ladies look and feel amazing. Honoring those who contribute to your life will surely bring them JOY.

What acts of kindness will you do for your celebrators?

_____
_____
_____
_____
_____
_____
_____
_____
_____

You Should Feel GOOD About Spreading Joy!

BRIDE-TO-BE TO DO LIST: (Check Off When Completed)

1.

2.

3.

4.

5.

THINK AND LIVE LIKE A BRIDE NOTES

_____

_____

_____

_____

_____

_____

_____

_____

_____

_____

_____

_____

_____

BRIDE-TO-BE TO DO LIST: (Check Off When Completed)

1.

2.

3.

4.

5.

THINK AND LIVE LIKE A BRIDE NOTES

_____
_____
_____
_____
_____
_____
_____
_____
_____
_____
_____
_____
_____
_____

BRIDE-TO-BE TO DO LIST: (Check Off When Completed)

1.

2.

3.

4.

5.

THINK AND LIVE LIKE A BRIDE NOTES

_____
_____
_____
_____
_____
_____
_____
_____
_____
_____
_____
_____
_____
_____

BRIDE-TO-BE TO DO LIST: (Check Off When Completed)

1.

2.

3.

4.

5.

THINK AND LIVE LIKE A BRIDE NOTES

_____
_____
_____
_____
_____
_____
_____
_____
_____
_____
_____
_____

BRIDE-TO-BE TO DO LIST: (Check Off When Completed)

1.

2.

3.

4.

5.

THINK AND LIVE LIKE A BRIDE NOTES

_____
_____
_____
_____
_____
_____
_____
_____
_____
_____
_____
_____
_____

BRIDE-TO-BE TO DO LIST: (Check Off When Completed)

1.

2.

3.

4.

5.

THINK AND LIVE LIKE A BRIDE NOTES

_____
_____
_____
_____
_____
_____
_____
_____
_____
_____
_____
_____

BRIDE-TO-BE TO DO LIST: (Check Off When Completed)

1.

2.

3.

4.

5.

THINK AND LIVE LIKE A BRIDE NOTES

_____

_____

_____

_____

_____

_____

_____

_____

_____

_____

_____

_____

BRIDE-TO-BE TO DO LIST: (Check Off When Completed)

1.

2.

3.

4.

5.

THINK AND LIVE LIKE A BRIDE NOTES

_____
_____
_____
_____
_____
_____
_____
_____
_____
_____
_____
_____
_____

BRIDE-TO-BE TO DO LIST: (Check Off When Completed)

1.

2.

3.

4.

5.

THINK AND LIVE LIKE A BRIDE NOTES

_____

_____

_____

_____

_____

_____

_____

_____

_____

_____

_____

_____

BRIDE-TO-BE TO DO LIST: (Check Off When Completed)

1.

2.

3.

4.

5.

THINK AND LIVE LIKE A BRIDE NOTES

_____

_____

_____

_____

_____

_____

_____

_____

_____

_____

_____

_____

MONTH 3 – TIME TO WRITE YOUR VOWS!

When the Bride and Groom are preparing for their wedding, they must decide on their wedding vows. The couple's wedding vows are recited at the ceremony to express their commitment and love for one another. I thought it would be appropriate for you to write vows for your life. When is the last time you promised yourself to be the best version of yourself? Well, today is the day that you get to have a guilt free day and think about how much you love you. I want you to THINK like a BRIDE in this exercise. Your VOWS to yourself should be from the heart.

I suggest starting with the first line as this:

I PROMISE TO LOVE MYSELF UNCONDITIONALLY. So many times we expect people to love us unconditionally when we don't do it for ourselves.

I PROMISE TO:

_____

_____

_____

I PROMISE TO:

_____

_____

_____

I PROMISE TO:

_____

_____

_____

CONGRATS! YOUR VOWS ARE ALL SET! NOW LIVE LIKE A BRIDE!

BRIDE-TO-BE TO DO LIST: (Check Off When Completed)

1.

2.

3.

4.

5.

THINK AND LIVE LIKE A BRIDE NOTES

_____
_____
_____
_____
_____
_____
_____
_____
_____
_____
_____
_____

BRIDE-TO-BE TO DO LIST: (Check Off When Completed)

1.

2.

3.

4.

5.

THINK AND LIVE LIKE A BRIDE NOTES

_____
_____
_____
_____
_____
_____
_____
_____
_____
_____
_____
_____
_____
_____

BRIDE-TO-BE TO DO LIST: (Check Off When Completed)

1.

2.

3.

4.

5.

THINK AND LIVE LIKE A BRIDE NOTES

_____
_____
_____
_____
_____
_____
_____
_____
_____
_____
_____
_____
_____

BRIDE-TO-BE TO DO LIST: (Check Off When Completed)

1.

2.

3.

4.

5.

THINK AND LIVE LIKE A BRIDE NOTES

_____
_____
_____
_____
_____
_____
_____
_____
_____
_____
_____
_____
_____

BRIDE-TO-BE TO DO LIST: (Check Off When Completed)

1.

2.

3.

4.

5.

THINK AND LIVE LIKE A BRIDE NOTES

_____
_____
_____
_____
_____
_____
_____
_____
_____
_____
_____
_____

BRIDE-TO-BE TO DO LIST: (Check Off When Completed)

1.

2.

3.

4.

5.

THINK AND LIVE LIKE A BRIDE NOTES

_____

_____

_____

_____

_____

_____

_____

_____

_____

_____

_____

_____

BRIDE-TO-BE TO DO LIST: (Check Off When Completed)

1.

2.

3.

4.

5.

THINK AND LIVE LIKE A BRIDE NOTES

_____

_____

_____

_____

_____

_____

_____

_____

_____

_____

_____

_____

_____

BRIDE-TO-BE TO DO LIST: (Check Off When Completed)

1.

2.

3.

4.

5.

THINK AND LIVE LIKE A BRIDE NOTES

_____

_____

_____

_____

_____

_____

_____

_____

_____

_____

_____

_____

_____

BRIDE-TO-BE TO DO LIST: (Check Off When Completed)

1.

2.

3.

4.

5.

THINK AND LIVE LIKE A BRIDE NOTES

_____
_____
_____
_____
_____
_____
_____
_____
_____
_____
_____
_____
_____

BRIDE-TO-BE TO DO LIST: (Check Off When Completed)

1.

2.

3.

4.

5.

_____
_____
_____
_____
_____
_____
_____
_____
_____
_____
_____
_____

MONTH 2 – LET'S HAVE SOME FUN

BRIDE-TO-BE... You deserve to have some FUN. You've been working on yourself for some time now. This next exercise can be done alone or with your **BRIDE TRIBE**; it's up to you. When I think about a wedding, I always think of the FUN activities that happen leading up to the Big Day. For example, the wedding shower, the games, the gifts, the shopping, rehearsal dinner, … Everybody deserves a Girls Day Out!

First things First, you deserve a shopping spree! Why? You've worked hard to **"Think and Live Like A Bride."** You've lost some emotional weight and even some physical weight as well. Go buy yourself a beautiful pair of earrings or purchase those dreamy pair of shoes that you will celebrate with in just a few days. I guarantee you that it will bring you some JOY. This is a QUILT FREE DAY! ENJOY.

What Did you Splurge On Today?

_____

_____

_____

PREPARE TO BE PAMPERED

Your family and friends are so proud of you. They see that you have been working hard to become the BEST version of you. You deserve to be celebrated not only on your BIG DAY, but every day moving forward. Don't feel guilty about all the love and attention that will come your way. You've positioned yourself to be pampered. It started with YOU committing to LOVE yourself unconditionally. You're now ready to receive all the LOVE that you deserve and have been waiting for.

IT'S GAME DAY!

Every **BRIDE-TO-BE** looks forward to the **Wedding Bridal Shower**. It's the day when your **BRIDE TRIBE** is ready to celebrate you with love, gifts, food, and **GAMES**! I'm laughing even as I type this, because some of those games can be embarrassing but FUN. Life can be stressful, but it doesn't have to be. Make sure to incorporate some fun and games into your life. One of my favorite games at any type of shower is **BINGO.** There are so many ways to play and win. I enjoy learning so much about the honoree.

Let's play **B.I.N.G.O.** and discover some things about YOU! Feel in the blanks and share information about you that you don't share often. Are you ready?

THINK AND LIVE LIKE A BRIDE BINGO ©

B Is For BEAUTY. Every BRIDE or BRIDE=TO-BE should feel beautiful about themselves. Talk about your beauty and how you value the beauty you have.

_____

_____

_____

I Is For INTEGRITY. One of the most important attributes you can have is Integrity. How do you live your life with Integrity?

_____

_____

_____

_____

N Is For Never. There are some things that you've promised NEVER to do again. For example, I will NEVER devalue who I am. Talk about it below.

_____

_____

_____

_____

_____

G Is For GRACE. We shared some about giving yourself GRACE. How will you extend GRACE to yourself and others?

_____

_____

_____

_____

_____

_____

O Is For Opportunities. Now that you are Open for Opportunities, how will you embrace them?

_____

_____

_____

_____

I want you to SHOUT the Word B.I.N.G.O. Why? Because you are a WINNER!
You're winning your RACE and it shows. Pat yourself on the back and say Good Job!

This GAME of **Think And Live Like A Bride B.I.N.G.O.** © should be shared with your
BRIDE TRIBE as well. You should want your Celebrators to be on the same JOY
JOURNEY as you.

BRIDE-TO-BE TO DO LIST: (Check Off When Completed)

1.

2.

3.

4.

5.

THINK AND LIVE LIKE A BRIDE NOTES

_____

_____

_____

_____

_____

_____

_____

_____

_____

_____

_____

_____

BRIDE-TO-BE TO DO LIST: (Check Off When Completed)

1.

2.

3.

4.

5.

THINK AND LIVE LIKE A BRIDE NOTES

_____

_____

_____

_____

_____

_____

_____

_____

_____

_____

_____

_____

BRIDE-TO-BE TO DO LIST: (Check Off When Completed)

1.

2.

3.

4.

5.

THINK AND LIVE LIKE A BRIDE NOTES

_____

_____

_____

_____

_____

_____

_____

_____

_____

_____

_____

_____

BRIDE-TO-BE TO DO LIST: (Check Off When Completed)

1.

2.

3.

4.

5.

THINK AND LIVE LIKE A BRIDE NOTES

BRIDE-TO-BE TO DO LIST: (Check Off When Completed)

1.

2.

3.

4.

5.

THINK AND LIVE LIKE A BRIDE NOTES

_____
_____
_____
_____
_____
_____
_____
_____
_____
_____
_____
_____
_____
_____
_____

BRIDE-TO-BE TO DO LIST: (Check Off When Completed)

1.

2.

3.

4.

5.

THINK AND LIVE LIKE A BRIDE NOTES

BRIDE-TO-BE TO DO LIST: (Check Off When Completed)

1.

2.

3.

4.

5.

THINK AND LIVE LIKE A BRIDE NOTES

_____
_____
_____
_____
_____
_____
_____
_____
_____
_____
_____
_____

BRIDE-TO-BE TO DO LIST: (Check Off When Completed)

1.

2.

3.

4.

5.

THINK AND LIVE LIKE A BRIDE NOTES

BRIDE-TO-BE TO DO LIST: (Check Off When Completed)

1.

2.

3.

4.

5.

THINK AND LIVE LIKE A BRIDE NOTES

_____

_____

_____

_____

_____

_____

_____

_____

_____

_____

_____

_____

BRIDE-TO-BE TO DO LIST: (Check Off When Completed)

1.

2.

3.

4.

5.

_____

_____

_____

_____

_____

_____

_____

_____

_____

_____

_____

_____

MONTH 1 – ALMOST DONE!

BRIDE-TO-BE, it's the Countdown to the BIG DAY! Can you believe that you are here? You've traveled through some storms and rain, sunshine, and pain to get here, but it's all a part of the Journey to JOY! You should be TICKLED PINK, BLUE, GREEN... or whatever your favorite color is. You did the work and now it's time to CELEBRATE! Well, ALMOST. Let's do a couple more things before the BIG DAY. I want you to be sure you're ready for this new place.

In a traditional wedding, the **BRIDE-TO-BE** will have to encounter new people and delegate certain responsibilities to them so that she is not overwhelmed. There is no way she can do it all. In this new place that you are in, you will have to Trust those who are assigned to your life. Trust is key when it comes to maintaining new relationships. Every person that comes into your life will have a purpose and role. When your life is full of JOY, you will attract Joyful people. Embrace this new place and the new people who will enhance your life as well.

BAD HAIR DAYS

I am not here to sell you a dream that you can't achieve. You can live a life of JOY, bad hair days and all. You know what a Bad Hair Day can do to a girl right? I've been there many times. It can potentially steal your joy and ruin your day. I'm sure you've experienced that as well. The curls didn't last because of the wind and rain. However, this is what I know for sure; Every Day is NOT a Bad Hair Day. The SUN will come out tomorrow... If we can apply that principle to our life, we will experience more JOY. Every day may not go as planned, but there's always tomorrow or another hour coming to make up for the time you think you lost. Keep planning your life with extraordinary JOY. How will you FIX your Bad Hair Day Experience?

_____

_____

_____

_____

_____

TIME FOR YOUR FITTING

Every **BRIDE-TO-BE** should have a FINAL FITTING before the Big Day. This fitting is to ensure that everything still fits the Bride. The Bride doesn't want any surprises on their special day. They want the dress to still fit as beautifully as it did when she received that final fitting a few months ago. Well, in life, we should have occasional fittings. How do you do that? Simply make sure your life is working for you. So often we ensure that we are there for everyone else, making sure that their life is in order. But when we fail to check-in with our own selves, we realize that some things are just not working. Make sure you have a mental check-in occasionally. Re-evaluate the people who are in your BRIDE TRIBE. Are they still loyal to you and are you to them as well? Did you remove negativity out of your life? Are you really living in JOY to the best of your ability? You'll be surprised at the alterations you will need to make to ensure your life is being lived to your standards. Don't be afraid to DETOX all the things necessary for your life to THRIVE. **Share below what areas need to be altered in your life.**

_____

_____

_____

_____

Share what IS WORKING in your life. You should be excited about your Joy Journey!

_____
_____
_____
_____
_____
_____
_____
_____
_____
_____

LAST MINUTE DETAILS

Something Old, Something New, Something Borrowed, Something Blue

BRIDE-TO-BE – You are almost ready to make that walk down the JOY aisle of life. You've been working, learning, and growing. You should be so proud of yourself and the results you see. Every **BRIDE-TO-BE** has last minute details they have do before the BIG DAY! Let's look at some of them.

SOMETHING OLD

Symbolizes Continuity With Family & Heritage

It's true that your family and close friends have been so incredibly supportive of your JOY Journey. You have so much to be grateful for. These are the people who understand that not every day has gone as planned, but they were patient and stood in your corner no matter what. Remember them with something special, such as a thank you card, gift or just words of gratitude.

SOMETHING NEW

Symbolizes A Bright Future

You are already enjoying your journey to JOY, and it shows. Something new doesn't have to be something you purchase. I bet you can find new things within you. For example, it's evident that your SMILE is bigger and brighter! What about your confidence level? You should be more confident about your life and the decisions you are making. It's something NEW and you should ENJOY this NEW YOU!

SOMETHING BORROWED

Symbolizes Wisdom From Experience

If you think about it, you've been borrowing WISDOM all along this JOY journey. You've learned from watching others and gleaning from people who know what it means to plan a life filled with JOY. I often think of Grandmothers, Mothers, Aunties and Friends who have poured into me so that I can become the BEST version of myself. Who have you borrowed wisdom from these past 12 months? How has it impacted your life? Take some time to think about it and share below.

_____

_____

_____

_____

_____

SOMETHING BLUE

Symbolizes Purity Of The Mind

One thing is certain on this journey and that is that your MIND has been decluttered. You are no longer carrying the weight of others and extra baggage that you were also trying to bring with you on this journey. You're so FREE to be YOU. In fact, go ahead and say, "I'm FREE To Be ME."

How do you feel about the journey thus far? Share below.

_____

_____

_____

_____

_____

_____

_____

_____

_____

_____

_____

_____

_____

TIME TO TAKE THE WALK

THE BIG DAY IS FINALLY HERE! Can you believe that you are here? Grab your Fancy dress or pant suit, bathing suit… Whatever makes you happy! LOL Remember that splurge day you had, and you purchased something special just for you? Grab that too and dress up! It's the day for which you've been waiting. Today, you are the **BRIDE!** You've been **Thinking Like A Bride so you can LIVE like the beautiful BRIDE you are!** No matter where your journey has taken you in life, you deserve this special day!

Before you gather your **BRIDE TRIBE**, take one last look in the mirror. You should be smiling at the reflection you see looking back at you. Today is _NOT_ the day to think about what could have been. Today you should be thinking on all the lovely things that relate to your life.

ALRIGHT, HERE COMES THE BRIDE!

LOOK AT YOU! All eyes are on you now. You've made some significant changes and it shows. You deserve all the attention you are receiving right now. It's your special day and you should take full advantage of it. Gather your BRIDE TRIBE and Celebrate! Slowly but eagerly walk into your NEW season of JOY. As you walk, with each step, be grateful for this journey. As you inhale deeply, EXHALE knowing that each breath is valuable. Today, nothing else matters, only your happiness. You are beautifully, fearfully, and wonderfully made. You light up the room with your presence. You're wearing the fragrance resilience and strength, mixed with gratefulness and kindness. The paparazzi are capturing your true beauty today and the crowd is in awe of the elegance you are displaying. Your GLAM Squad consists of Faith, Peace, Hope and Determination. Each plays a significant role as to where it is placed in your life. You understand just how much of each is needed daily to keep this JOY. This JOY that you have wasn't given to you by anyone. You looked within and FOUND out it was there all along. And since no one gave it to you, no one can take it away. It's a GIFT that will be yours forever.

CONGRATULATIONS BRIDE! YOU DID IT.

NOW LIVE LIKE THE BRIDE YOU ARE!

JUST IN CASE... YOU'RE PLANNING A BIG DAY (ANY SPECIAL EVENT) HERE'S A QUICK CHECK LIST FOR YOU.

9 TO 12 MONTHS PRIOR TO BIG DAY:

- ☐ Arrange a gathering for you, your parents, and the entire **BRIDE TRIBE.**
- ☐ Determine budget and how expenses will be shared.
- ☐ Discuss the size, style, location, and scope of the wedding you want.
- ☐ Choose a target event date and time. (The actual date will depend on venue availability.)
- ☐ Create a binder to store and organize ideas, worksheets, receipts, brochures, etc.
- ☐ Visit and reserve wedding/special event and reception sites.
- ☐ Meet with your officiant or coordinator.
- ☐ Start compiling your guest list to estimate head count. Consider budget when thinking about "must-invites" versus "nice-to-invites."
- ☐ Begin shopping for the wedding gown or special outfit/accessories.

6 TO 9 MONTHS PRIOR:

- ☐ Choose the members of your Bride Tribe (Celebrators ONLY).
- ☐ Enroll in wedding/shower gift registries if applicable.
- ☐ Hire a photographer and a videographer.
- ☐ Book an engagement photo session, especially if you plan to include a professional engagement picture with Save-the-Date cards.
- ☐ Hire a caterer.
- ☐ Hire a florist.
- ☐ Make arrangements for music to be played at the ceremony and reception. (Tasks might include booking a band or solo musician, hiring a DJ, choosing significant musical selections, and so on.).
- ☐ Reserve a block of hotel rooms for out-of-town guests. (Ask about group rates.)

- ☐ Send out Save-the-Date cards. (Include lodging info and maps, as possible.)

- ☐ Shop for wedding rings or your special gift for YOU.

- ☐ Select and order wedding gown or special outfit, leaving ample time for delivery and alterations.

- ☐ Shop for bridesmaids' dresses.

- ☐ Schedule cake design appointments and tastings.

- ☐ Start planning your honeymoon or special trip. (How Fun this will be)

4 TO 6 MONTHS PRIOR:

- ☐ Finalize the guest list.

- ☐ Order invitations (25 extra) and other wedding stationery (i.e., place cards and thank you notes).

- ☐ Plan wedding or special day beauty preparations; ask your stylist how far in advance they book wedding or special parties, and whether they are willing to work on the site.

- ☐ Finalize all travel plans. If traveling outside the country, arrange for visas, passports, and inoculations.

- ☐ Hire your wedding/special day transportation (carriage, limousine service, etc.).

- ☐ Plan the rehearsal dinner.

2 TO 4 MONTHS PRIOR:

- ☐ Obtain a marriage license if applicable. Bring all necessary documents.

- ☐ Order tuxedoes for the groom and groomsmen.

- ☐ Meet with the caterer to go over menus, wine selections, etc.

- ☐ Order the special cake.

- ☐ Order your wedding rings or special jewelry.

- ☐ Confirm wedding/special event ceremony and reception music.

- ☐ Book a hotel room for the wedding night or just because you deserve it!

- ☐ If you plan to write your own vows, start writing them now.

4 TO 8 WEEKS PRIOR:

- [ ] Mail the invitations 8 weeks before your event date.

- [ ] Do a hair and makeup run-through (including wedding veil, if applicable).

- [ ] Confirm all transportation plans.

2 TO 4 WEEKS PRIOR:

- [ ] Work on seating arrangements for the reception.

- [ ] Finalize arrangements for out-of-town attendants and guests.

- [ ] Confirm details with the photographer, florist, and other vendors.

- [ ] Have final fitting for wedding gown and bridesmaids' dresses if needed.

- [ ] Write your rehearsal dinner toast.

- [ ] Purchase gifts for the wedding attendants. (If applicable)

- [ ] Compile a list of all the wedding/special event vendors and wedding party, with contact information. Carry this list with you everywhere you go (just in case).

- [ ] Communicate rehearsal dinner details to those who will attend the rehearsal and rehearsal dinner.

- [ ] Look into where bride, groom and attendants will dress for the ceremony.

1 WEEK PRIOR:

- [ ] Enclose any fees due on the wedding day in envelopes for easy distribution.

- [ ] Appoint someone to act as an "organizer" to handle any last-minute problems.

- [ ] Give the caterer a final head count.
- [ ] Appoint a trustworthy person to bring important items (cake knife, toasting glasses, etc.) to the reception.
- [ ] Review final details for those in the wedding party.
- [ ] Get final beauty treatments (manicure, facial, massage, waxing, brow shaping, etc.)

THE DAY BEFORE THE BIG DAY:

- [ ] Confirm travel arrangements.
- [ ] Pack for the honeymoon or trip.
- [ ] Enjoy a relaxing day with family and friends.
- [ ] Attend the rehearsal and rehearsal dinner; give gifts to attendants, if applicable.
- [ ] Give the rings, and officiant's fee, to the best man. (If applicable).
- [ ] Try to get some rest

THE BIG DAY:

- [ ] Post wedding announcements or BIG DAY announcements in the mail.
- [ ] Relax and remain calm.
- [ ] Remember to eat something.
- [ ] Allow at least two hours for getting dressed.

ENJOY YOUR SPECIAL DAY!